CHRISTIAN PASTORS, TRAIN THE LOCAL CHURCH TO MAKE DISCIPLES OF JESUS

How the mission, message, and man of the gospel transforms pastoral ministry and leadership.

Copyright © 2020 Mr. Nate Gunter

Published by TGJS Publishing

All rights reserved. This book or any portion thereof may not be reproduced or used in any manner whatsoever without the express written permission of the publisher except for the use of brief quotations in a book review.

Printed in the United States of America

First Printing, 2020

ISBN 9780578720616 (Print/Paperback)
ISBN 9780578720647 (eBook)

Updates, more books, resources, and related information available at: www.MrNateBooks.com

TABLE OF CONTENTS

Dedication 1

Preface 2

Chapter 1: Introduction 5

Chapter 2: Training to Make Disciples Because of
    Jesus' Teaching 14
    Jesus Teaching as the God-Man 15
    Jesus Teaching because of the Mission 19
    Jesus Teaching by the Message 23

Chapter 3: Training to Make Disciples Because of
    Jesus' Example 30
    Example through Jesus' Communication 33
    Example by Jesus' Life 38

Chapter 4: Training to Make Disciples Because of
    Jesus' Redemption 49
    Jesus Redeems a Pastor 53
    Prayer 55
    Reading the Word 57
    Jesus Redeems a Pastor's Mission 63

Chapter 5: Conclusion 69
    Implications for a Pastor's Teaching 70
    Applications for a Pastor's Example 71

Bibliography 75

About The Author 78

DEDICATION

To my parents for enduring pastoral ministry over 40 years after ending his athletic career and high hopes for successful baseball future to follow Christ into pastoral ministry -- often without the glamor or glory. It was not always pretty or fun but worth it. My mom served in different capacities like Sunday school teacher, during the time I heard the gospel through flannel graphs among bus ministry kid crowds brought from all over our Sacramento, CA city region to hear God's word.

PREFACE

This book comes from my graduate, seminary school days when working through the end of my degree. It's been slightly re-formatted and edited, and it provides a summary dive into the topic of pastoral ministry – mainly the purpose. I purposely chose to write on a subject I would be personally be involved with and continue in for a lifetime as the Lord willed. There are countless issues and items to address in pastoral ministry from counseling life situations, how to preach and teach, how to budget personally or corporately, officiate weddings and funerals, what to do with "ministries," what are the biblical ways to "govern" a local church, and so on that this book does not address directly though will be affected by it. This would be a book I use as a tool for training people initially learning about pastoral ministry or a reminder to those that are pastors of the original profound simplicity of Jesus and the gospel in pastoral ministry.

Christian Pastors, Train the Local Church to Make Disciples of Jesus

I grew up as a double PK, pastor's kid and principle's kid, as my dad started a local church and Christian school. Later in my life from high school through college, my athletic career changed to pastoral. The clearest thing that happened in my life was the clarity and certainty of the gospel for real life, especially that of pastoring. I have served among several churches in various capacities and ages, from cleaning toilets to pastoring. Some say there's correlation to those two jobs and it makes me laugh. God seems to have built a lot more elements of pastoring and perspective into my life. He placed me in a job during seminary that dealt directly with thousands of pastors and churches across the nation. I've also worked several different, non-pastor and non-Christian jobs providing a wide array of relationships and view of the world and people. I have also researched numerous books, old and new, about pastoring along with being involved directly with pastors and churches personally and researching their history.

I love pastoring. I love people. And, I love God. None of that is perfect, but he is and I trust that for myself, my family, and for others. God is the best pastor anyone can have, especially for pastors. As David says using some old school KJV translation I grew up with of Psalms 23:1 and 3, "The Lord is my shepherd; I shall not want ... Yea, though I walk through the valley of the shadow of death, I will fear no evil: for thou art with me; thy rod and staff they comfort me."

I certainly have seen the viciousness of the world and the church beyond God's natural world of beauty. I have seen churches crumble, split, combine, strain, plateau, decline, erode, compromise, change, disband, grow, and fight. I have seen churches do good and great things, even making the gospel clear. I have seen churches underpay pastors and communities lack financial generosity, creating an awful scenario for pastors to survive and having to work several jobs. I have seen churches provide well for pastors, their families, and even international missionaries.

One thing remains true for any person, especially pastors – God. Live for him and you will find yourself in the eye of the storm. Jesus truly is good news – the gospel for real life. Shepherd people to him.

CHAPTER 1

INTRODUCTION

What is the primary goal for a pastor in the local church? Is the goal to be the "one-man ministry"[1] doing all of the ministry work such as hospital visits, preaching, evangelism, funerals, weddings, study, small groups or even Sunday school? Or is it to multiply pastors to spread the help? Or is to emphasize preaching in an effort to "feed" God's people truth?[2] Or is it to run a

---

[1] The authors supply solutions to replace a one-man team. Derek Prime and Alistair Begg, *On Being a Pastor: Understanding Our Calling and Work* (Chicago, IL: Moody, 2004), 238. C.f Robert E. Coleman, *The Master Plan of Discipleship* (Old Tappan, N.J.: Revell, 1987), 81.

[2] Though not opposed to other goals and objectives to the pastorate, MacArthur places primary emphasis to preaching and teaching within the role and function of the pastorate. John MacArthur, *Pastoral Ministry: What Is a Pastor to Be and Do?* (Nashville, TN: Thomas Nelson, 2005), 15.

non-profit, volunteer organization? Or is it to do something else besides "secular work?" Or is it to create a brand and trend or even keep old traditions? These options form a mere few of countless options pastors find themselves in when entering and continuing in pastoral ministry. Often these options arise to prominent pastoral goals that create a pastoral goal pendulum.

A pastor living by the one-man ministry principle may burnout[3] sooner than later and even fail the church being incapable of fulfilling all the responsibilities. Pastors living by the multi-pastor pattern can fall prey to strength and authority in numbers that often leverage accountability as means of control or power struggles. A pastor living by the emphasis on preaching may fall into the trap of not fulfilling other pastoral duties and even leading the flock to be merely eaters of knowledge than exercising. These goals among others lead the local church to become passive in their responsibilities and exercising spiritual gifts or overtly trained to become

---

[3] May include spiritual, physical, emotional and even familial health.

"churchy" or "religious." Often the "church" is known as a property, address, website, and group of people to govern and lead versus people that form community along with people within the vicinity, including personal vicinity of the pastor(s). Does God see things or people?

The one-man ministry attempts to complete all of the ministry responsibilities, leaving the members nothing to do as if they are on vacation. The multi-pastor attracts similarity or diversity to the current group to be the entrance into governance which creates awkwardly forming leadership groups that have nothing to do with scripture but comfortability or cultural definitions. The emphasis on preaching leads the members to be like fattened sheep with no exercise, lending many times to an arrogant attitude towards others, especially to skinnier sheep. The focus on trendy trains people's attention to be on the present time and culture. The tradition training keeps focus on all things in the past. The organizational entity training builds a behemoth of tasks, often unrelated to real life claiming "real life impact" like "look how much good we are doing in the community." These approaches to the pastorate is reflected through the church's culture as in "attitudes, customs, and beliefs that distinguish one group of people from another."[4]

What do we want people to be following? Merely one pastor, several pastors, an organizational entity, a trend, a tradition, or even themselves through selfish ambitions? What do we want these people to become? Passive, bloated on Bible knowledge, concerned for image, controlled by culture, controlled by tradition, or even misdirected talent? What do we want out of their lives? Focused on a weekly 1-3 hours of church life or of what God wants for the entirety of their life?

These questions dig into the primary task of pastors to be either guiding and training people to be followers of something else or of Jesus. We have two thousand years worth of evidence of both failure and success of what it means to be a pastor, and more so, a

---

[4] Robert Lewis and Wayne Cordeiro, *Culture Shift Transforming Your Church from the inside Out* (San Francisco, CA: Jossey-Bass, 2005), 12.

Christian. For the American church, we have at least 50-75 years of examples and evidence of how people have been trained to follow Christ. Often Christianity seems to be focused on so much beyond what's in the name, "Christ." Determining the pastor's goal in the church is essential for properly influencing and directing anyone, especially the Christian church to live in obedience to Jesus Christ.

Jesus Christ in the Great Commission left his disciples and all subsequent believers one primary command[5] to obey, which is to "make disciples."[6] Making disciples was not a foreign concept during Jesus' time and a task that Jesus modeled. Making disciples refers to "calling individuals to absolute commitment to the person of Jesus as one's sole Master and Lord."[7] Jesus called people to follow him through

---

[5] Inclusive of the two primary commands of love God and love your neighbor. C.f. Luke 10:27 and Deuteronomy 6:5.

[6] Matthew 28:18-20; Acts 1:6-8.

[7] Continual process including both point of salvation and life thereafter. Michael J. Wilkins, *The NIV Application Commentary: Matthew*, ed. Terry Muck (Grand Rapids, MI: Zondervan, 2004), 952.

his teaching and example. All who Jesus is, said, and did called people to become disciples. These disciples make disciples by imitating Jesus in calling people through what they say and do. A disciple is a follower and a follower is a believer.[8] Since all believers make up the church[9] and are commanded by Jesus, making disciples is to permeate the church's culture. "What will our churches and ministries be like if we live out the message that the expectations of discipleship found in the Gospels are expectations for all Christians...?"[10]

To ensure that the church (people) lives out Jesus' message of making disciples, Jesus "gave" the church pastors "to equip the saints for the work of ministry."[11] "Equip" is used synonymously to train,[12] and

---

[8] Michael J. Wilkins, *Following the Master a Biblical Theology of Discipleship* (Grand Rapids, MI: Zondervan, 1992), 40.

[9] Edmund P. Clowney, *The Church* (Downers Grove, IL: Intervarsity, 1995), 28 and 47.

[10] Wilkins, *Following the Master a Biblical Theology of Discipleship*, 47.

[11] Ephesians 4:12.

"ministry" belonging to all believers encompasses Jesus' primary command of making disciples. The pastor's[13] primary goal is to follow Christ, which then is to make that clear as a primary command to all believers a reality through training them. This training actively sets making disciples into the DNA of the church. Training is communicating what to believe (teaching) and demonstrating how to apply teaching (example) for believers to follow in order to accomplish the ministry.

Since following Christ is the primary goal of a Christian and a command for any peoples of the world, then making disciples becomes intrinsically and inextricably connected to all believers. Pastors are to already be personally in the process of doing just that, making disciples, which includes the relational engagement and interaction of unbelievers or non-Christians. Training merely includes others to observe

---

[12] C.f. further detailed exegetical discussion in using "training" or "preparing." Harold W. Hoehner, *Ephesians an Exegetical Commentary* (Grand Rapids, MI: Baker, 2002), 550.

[13] Regardless of spiritual gift or office.

and participate in making disciples to be able to do on their own. Jesus, being the chief shepherd[14] (pastor), is and acts as the greatest example and reason for a pastor's primary goal of personally following Christ and training the local church to make disciples.

People within the local church see, hear, and know a pastor, especially what he represents. A pastor is to represent Jesus, full of grace and truth, who denied himself, took up his cross, followed God the Father by the power of the Holy Spirit which inevitably and purposely made disciples to do likewise. When the pastor does so and faithfully trains others (and assuming people receive the training), the church's culture transforms from sterile, hypocritical, judgmental, isolated, dissatisfied, divisive, heretical, or heartless to genuinely unified in following Jesus Christ by Christ himself being the epicenter of our hearts, history, and humanity.

---

[14] 1 Peter 5:4.

The following chapters outline chief pastor Jesus' teaching, example, and redemption in order to validate the reason behind a pastor's primary goal in following Christ and secondarily training the local church to make disciples. The particular writing style aims to be readable for an average lay leader and pastor.

Grammatical and exegetical work of passages is reflected through certain uses of English composition posed in each chapter (forms, tenses, etc.) to simplify reading and understanding of the texts. Various sources are referenced to best assist the reader to further develop and understand an outside perspective. What seems to be an overwhelming use of scriptures is important to reveal the immense, complex, but also simple understanding that the Bible clearly states the reason for pastors to train the local church to make disciples.

CHAPTER 2
TRAINING TO MAKE DISCIPLES BECAUSE OF JESUS' TEACHING

Jesus, being the master teacher, is the centerpiece and epicenter of wisdom[15] for training the local church to make disciples. Jesus stated, "when everyone is fully trained he will be like his teacher."[16] What part of Jesus' teaching trained his followers? Was it witty one-liners, parables, timing, personality, schedule, energy, or content? Yes, as it was not merely one thing but all of who he is. It was his person, mission, and message that trained his followers. The following reveals Jesus, the chief pastor, for pastors to trust and also imitate: (1) Jesus Teaching as the God-Man; (2) Jesus Teaching

---

[15] Colossians 2:3.
[16] Luke 6:40.

because of the Mission; and (3) Jesus Teaching by the Message.

Jesus Teaching as the God-Man

Throughout history, the Bible's teaching that Jesus Christ is both God and man has led many to confusion but also many to salvation. If Jesus is not both God and man, then he is not Jesus Christ of the Bible, nor is he a teacher for a pastor to follow. By not establishing Jesus' identity, character, and personality, whether ignorantly or purposely, one inevitably removes trust in him and his teaching.

Gnosticism, beginning in the early 1st century, established Jesus as merely a spiritual being, existing in a physical façade of a body. Gnostics denied Jesus to be God and human, which trained people to follow a false Jesus. Gnostics believed Jesus became a figurehead or teacher sent to the earth to proclaim salvific knowledge, revealing humans were once spiritually existing before earth in a different universe.[17] Astute pastors will conclude that Gnostics attempted to remove Jesus' divinity and humanity, thereby, removing his truthful message and misdirecting from the actual person and work of Jesus. Therefore, the pastor must establish who Jesus is to rightly believe, follow, and train.

Jesus proclaimed himself to be the promised one, the Christ, the Messiah, the anointed one, the elect one, the redeemer, the savior, and divinely the God of the Old Testament,[18] affirmed by John in describing Jesus divine as is God the Father and the Holy Spirit – 3 persons in 1 divine existence.[19] Though this may initially come across confusing to many and many teachers have tried various analogies that fall short and astray, one naturally serves to explain well – which is that of humanity and marriage. Meaning, a husband and wife

---

[17] Justo L. Gonzalez, *The Early Church to the Dawn of the Reformation*, vol. 1, 3 vols., The Story of Christianity (New York, NY: Harper Collins, 1984), 59-60.

[18] Exodus 3:14; John 8:58.

[19] John1:1. God as Trinity-God the Father, Son, and Spirit.

are known biblically two as one.[20] And in their "one flesh" they are still distinctly different people, man and woman. They share the same nature of human (i.e. not insect, animal, etc.), and they are distinct. Hence God is one nature and three distinct persons – the Father, Son, and Spirit – working as one, united, and equal though different. His creation follows him as the Creator, we are in his image though we are not him.[21]

Believing that God created all things and all peoples,[22] all peoples and specifically believers are under his will and authority, which demands us to listen and to obey His words.[23] The mere content of his teaching makes no difference if it is not connected to his divinity. As a pastor follows this line of belief and thinking, he will resolve to himself that Jesus is not just the source of teaching but the key part in the teaching.

---

[20] Genesis 2:24.

[21] Genesis 1:26 (c.f. Genesis 3:5).

[22] Genesis 1:1.

[23] John 3:36; 10:27.

Jesus' Humanity

Knowing Jesus Christ to be the God-man, the incarnate Son of God, leads a pastor to understand the immanence (not just transcendence) of God and his teaching.[24] Jesus, who is God, dwelt[25] among people in flesh on the earth. Gnostics attempted to remove this fact and approached Jesus in a dualistic fashion, placing Jesus in a distant and separate relationship to God and man.[26] Docetism rose in the early church, giving way to a heretical understanding of Jesus appearing to be human, rather than both divine and human flesh,[27] concluding God was never close to his creation.

A pastor must establish the truth of who Jesus is (both in his divinity and humanity) and also how

---

[24] John 1:14.

[25] Greek word for dwelt in John 1:14 also means and contains imagery of "tabernacled" -- referencing the tabernacle the remained and traveled with the Israelites during the Old Testament wilderness journey.

[26] D. Jeffrey Bingham, *Pocket History of the Church* (Downers Grove, IL: Intervarsity, 2002), 40-41.

[27] Ibid., 23.

Jesus relates to people because of who he is. Erring on either his person or relationship to creation depicts an unreal Jesus. Jesus made and trained disciples because of who he is, which is also to be descriptive of a pastor. If Jesus is relating closely to his creation to make them as disciples and also training them, then pastors are to do likewise.

Jesus Teaching because of the Mission

Jesus, because of who he is, determined who he followed: God the Father.[28] God the Father set the mission for Jesus to fulfill, which is focused on saving and calling the saved to follow the Father. Jesus took an active role that ensures the mission of saving and calling people is completed.[29]

---

[28] John 1:13; 5:30; 6:38.
[29] John 19:30.

The Father's Will

Jesus, because of who he is, helpfully and graciously guided sinful people to the one who set the mission, the Father.[30] Jesus came to complete the mission of offering the world salvation through his life, death, and resurrection. By doing so Jesus glorified God the Father as the one to be desired, obeyed, and pursued.[31] The overall life of Jesus, such as relationships, schedule, places, events, giving, and actions, models for a pastor a pattern of life both in word and deed intentional on fulfilling the Father's mission.

The Great Commission reveals then that the Father's mission included all believers partaking in making disciples since they are disciples of him. Jesus ensured the continuation of the Father's mission after his earthly ministry by equipping believers with both teaching and example. The goal of Jesus' teaching and example in the mission was two-fold and not separate

---

[30] John 6:44.
[31] John 17:1.

from one another: (1) make disciples and (2) train disciples. This two-fold goal is to become a main part of the pastor's personal and public life.

When pastors lack making disciples in their personal life, they are indirectly training the local church to be unaware and inconsistent in their obedience to Jesus. More so, the local church would then be trained to live an isolated life and never reaching the world for Jesus Christ, hence ignoring the Father's will and Jesus' mission.[32]

Salvation

The very nature and offer of salvation reveals God's heart for all peoples to follow him. He has provided an eternal, relational, perfect access to himself through Jesus.[33] Jesus bore the sins of the world and clothed those believing in him with his righteousness, thereby accepting them into his eternal, heavenly

---

[32] C.f. 1 Corinthians 9:22.
[33] John 3:16.

presence. Since God sought the world through Jesus, then pastors are to seek the world because of Jesus. Lacking any sort of training to make disciples, the church misses God, basic principles of the character of God, and God's love for all peoples. Pastors are to be a means for the church to know God and share in his love for the nations, which results in making disciples.

Therefore, pastors and people are God's program to affect the people around them relationally. When pastors attempt to "build" a church through programmatic means, often relationships and the message of Christ and Christianity become twisted or skewed. Then it becomes an invitation to church vs. an invitation to Christ. It becomes a schedule and performance focus vs. salvation to real life, that then shows up serving the church genuinely, lovingly, relationally, and soundly. Making disciples comes with a message for all to hear and see throughout real life with the central figure of Christ being the cornerstone of it all. If we become more focused on training people to be great members of churches, we may often be leading them astray from being great servants to Christ – whom they are suppose to be members.[34] What would we rather have, a signed document to be a member of an organizational entity of a local church or a saved person living their life for Christ without any need of signing a document because Christ's blood has already signed salvation and sanctification?

Jesus Teaching by the Message

Jesus, because of who he is, determined who he followed (God the Father), who he followed determined what he said, and what he said and did was helped by who empowered him (God the Spirit).[35] Dwelling among the peoples of the earth as the God-man, he commands an amazing, authoritative message for all to hear. Jesus taught his disciples how to reach the world for him, which is through the message and example.[36] The message proposes the need and solution,

---

[34] 1 Corinthians 6:15.

[35] John 7:17-18.

[36] Matthew 14:13-36, the parable of fish and loaves of bread where Jesus explains through message and action that he is the

whereas the example provides the validation of the message. Jesus taught through both his message and example.

Verbal Message

Jesus' message was verbal and direct. Though, seemingly unimportant to the average pastor or Bible reader, the very fact of verbalizing a message proves overwhelmingly important over time. At least two traps hinder a pastor from appropriately verbalizing even the gospel message. First, a pastor may offer merely motivational speeches containing information related to or completely unrelated to either the Bible or Jesus' teachings. Second, a pastor may believe that discipleship comes through a person seeing only actions, instead of additionally listening to a verbal message. The pastor's philosophy of ministry must not be limited to

---

sustenance and satisfaction for all people just as the fish and bread were broken into pieces to feed the thousands, so he will be through his life, death, and resurrection.

helping the poor,[37] praying for the sick[38] or giving to those in need.[39] Though throughout Scripture these are healthy works of a believer's faith in Jesus, nothing can remove or replace the command and need for verbalizing Jesus' message.[40]

Gospel Message

More importantly, the gospel message rises to the top of all messages to verbalize. Jesus spoke of himself as the savior, the one to follow, and the one to believe for eternal salvation and relationship with God the Father. Without the gospel message, the people of the world die in their sins separated from God for all eternity, which opposes God's purpose of sending Jesus to save the world. God does reserve wrath[41] for those that

---

[37] Matthew 19:21.

[38] James 5:14.

[39] 1 John 3:17.

[40] Romans 10:14.

[41] John 3:18.

lack belief and repentance; however, he equally reserves salvation through his grace, love, and mercy.[42]

Paul reminded even the Corinthian church, in the midst of utter sinful chaos, of the centrality of the gospel.[43] Paul evokes their memories of previous years in which he preached or verbalized the message to them. By this message the Corinthian church was to maintain unity and spiritual health. Paul does not support the idea of the gospel being a one-time message purely for salvation. Paul speaks of the verbalized gospel message as something to live by – a lifestyle. Without the gospel, without Jesus death and resurrection, Paul claims his verbalized message and the faith of his readers are both useless.[44] Jesus verbalized his message to his disciples about who he is and what they were to do with the truth of his message. His disciples were to have both a belief as well as an action from that belief, which is the very definition to the term "religious" or "religion." The

---

[42] John 3:16.

[43] 1 Corinthians 15:1-4.

[44] 1 Corinthians 15:14.

direct implication for the disciples was to repeat Jesus' message to others. The direct application for the disciples was to make disciples, an outflow of God's work in them to affect the world around them for his purposes. Hence why Paul describes Christians as "his workmanship."[45]

Dispersed Message

Paul also refers to the verbalized gospel message as both truth and historical (i.e. not just "spiritual"). The message became historical to Paul as Jesus died and rose again from the cross decades before writing 1 Corinthians.[46] The message had been transferred through witnesses of Jesus' resurrection to the generation born after Jesus' ascension.[47] The message also spread throughout areas geographically

---

[45] Ephesians 2:10

[46] 1 Corinthians 15:5-8.

[47] Luke 1:1-4; Acts 1:6-8. C.f. Hebrews 11 of the gospel applied to those previous to Jesus (i.e. Old Testament).

and proved to be a message of both salvation and disciple making.

During Jesus' earthly ministry, he affirmed to Peter that the church would hear the gospel through him and the other disciples.[48] Jesus is referring to Peter receiving him and his message, and then relaying the message to the world. As such, the message of Jesus would both transfer to the next generations and geographically around the world – a cycle of good news.

The greatest evidence for the transfer to the next generation and geographical locations is looking throughout the book of Acts. Jesus ended his earthly ministry with the Great Commission,[49] and the disciples began obedience to his commission. Peter launched a verbalized gospel message to those assembled together.[50] Three thousand of the assembly believed the message and came to salvation. Making disciples of all the world became the main focus for Jesus' disciples following his

---

[48] Matthew 16:18.
[49] Matthew 28:18-20.
[50] Acts 2:14-41.

ascension, with the proposed expanse of the gospel message[51] and Peter's sermon. The remaining chapters in Acts reveals the disciples making disciples of all previously proposed geographical regions such as Israel, Asia Minor, Greece, Africa, and even Rome.

Understanding that Jesus both desired and planned his message to be verbalized and spread dynamically sets one's philosophy of ministry. By the very nature of the message, pastors are to disperse this message to the local area as well as the local church. The pastor must train the local church to spread the message as well, just as Jesus did with his disciples. Therefore, pastors verbally teach the actual message and also train the church how to teach others, rather than taking on the dispersion single handedly.

---

[51] Acts 1:8.

CHAPTER 3
TRAINING TO MAKE DISCIPLES BECAUSE OF JESUS' EXAMPLE

Jesus validated his verbalized message of salvation to the world through being an example.[52] Jesus made clear to the disciples and followers how to make disciples in word and also in deed. Jesus expressed and manifested an extraordinary example for pastors to follow even today. Jesus did not live a hypocritical life or present a dichotomy between person and work. His example showed his words.

It's difficult to pastor people and issues arise throughout the tenure of a pastor, hence why the need to focus on Jesus is critical. Sometimes what pastors do conflicts with what they say, right or wrong, through

---

[52] John 13:14.

these pastoral pressures. Sometimes they are brought on by their own decision-making and sometimes they are genuinely trying to help. Sometimes people respond horribly and others attracted to personality, organizational benefits ("they have a great kid's ministry"), and the list continues. Pastors can fall prey to certain situations among others. Like, a one-man ministry stresses that the example is to only be of himself and no one else. A multi-pastor leadership stresses the biblical context for governing and focus on local church submission to doctrinal statements, bylaws, membership, schedules, and involvement in the organizational structure entity. A pulpit preacher stresses the content, structure, and delivery of a message rather than any personal life demonstration to the message's validity. An organizational pastor trains volunteers to program and seeks a cyclical hype culture for people's motivation to stay engaged. A traditional pastor keeps focus on the old ways and styles of "the way it used to be" as a more righteous option than others. A trendy pastor stays up with the cultural trends of the world and church ministry often diminishing teaching God's word for real life.

Though Jesus taught knowledge, "knowledge unapplied to living can become a stumbling stone to further truth."[53] Jesus taught by word and example, which led people to faith in him and not merely his words -- hence why Jesus is known as the living word.[54] Jesus did not create organizational structures, programs, or ministries rather his serving others was a direct result of who he was and he stewarded things for the sake of the primary goal and glory of God. He trained disciples by how he made disciples, which was not directing them in how to be better schedulers, organizers, or church leaders though there was scheduling, organizing, and leadership along with constant changes. He directed them to listen and learn from what he modeled which resulted in a change of heart, character, and relationship which is often overlooked. He modeled following God the Father by the empowerment of the Spirit. It's not that

---

[53] Coleman, *The Master Plan of Discipleship*, 69.
[54] John 1:1-5.

things and organization are bad, but when we prioritize the things and even people, we de-value and diminish the priority of the gospel and being a follower of him.

Jesus modeled what pastors are to strive towards, which is a unified life proclaiming the gospel in word and in example. Jesus' followers listened to him as he continued to validate his words, proving to the disciples his divinity and humanity as the God-man on mission, fulfilling God the Father's will. A pastor must conclude that his own person and character must not be devoid of this work in making disciples. The following two categories will assist the pastor in understanding Jesus' example sets the basis of the why and how in training the local church to make disciples: (1) Example through Jesus' Communication and (2) Example by Jesus' Life.

Example through Jesus' Communication

Jesus' words communicated with authority reflected his mission. A pastor needs to ask, did Jesus speak in a manner that arrogantly belittled the people around him because he had authoritative truth? It seemed as if he had the right to do so because of their sin, but evidently he approached communication to the people differently. Jesus' disciples lived along with him learning or being trained by his example of communicating to people the truth.

Jesus' Authority

By Jesus' authority he commissioned his disciples to make disciples of the world.[55] Jesus' authority forgave people of their sins,[56] delivered people from demons,[57] rebuked hypocrites,[58] gave life to unbelievers,[59] controlled nature,[60] encouraged patience during trials,[61] proclaimed God's words,[62] rebuked

---

[55] Matthew 28:18-20.
[56] Luke 5:20.
[57] Luke 4:33.
[58] Luke 6:42.
[59] John 16:27.
[60] Matthew 8:26.
[61] Matthew 26:52.
[62] Matthew 4:4.

Satan,[63] healed the sick,[64] raised the dead,[65] and even ate with sinners.[66] Though not an exhaustive list, it displays how Jesus used his authority. Jesus did not rule as a Roman soldier wielding his sword to slay sinners, nor passive nature that never confronts issues. Jesus rightly used his authority because of his character and nature. He dealt with those around him in a manner consistent with his loving, merciful, gracious, and just nature. He used his authority to communicate himself as the "way, truth and life."[67]

Jesus' Words

Along with Jesus' authority came forth his words.[68] Jesus possessed every right to walk among the people rebuking all of their sins, mainly unbelief or

---

[63] Matthew 4:7.
[64] Luke 4:40.
[65] John 11:43.
[66] Mark 2:16.
[67] John 14:6.
[68] John 17:14.

rejection of him. Jesus, the centerpiece of wisdom,[69] chose to use his everyday words to reveal to people who he is and how he loves them. Jesus chose words to graciously forgive and withhold wrath from an adulterous woman, and at the same time rebuke the scribes and Pharisees for their misguided and condemning words toward her.[70]

Jesus revealed to his disciples that words matter to those around them. By these words, they will make disciples. By misusing words, the disciples may certainly guide people away from Jesus. Even though Jesus has all authority and the right to use harsh words to the world, he used this right to guide people to him and trained his disciples to do likewise.[71] "Disciples spent time with their master and became learning sponges, soaking up the teaching and example of the one from

---

[69] Colossians 1:28-29.
[70] John 8:3-11.
[71] Matthew 10:16.

whom they were learning."[72] Pastors are sponges to their chief pastor, Jesus.

Jesus' Mission

Jesus communicated his mission.[73] He made it extremely clear to his disciples, though the disciples struggled many times grasping with the fact that he was to die and rise again.[74] Even Peter desired for Jesus to stay alive rather than fulfilling the mission.[75] Jesus communicated the mission with authoritative words. Jesus set the tone and direction for the disciples to take after his ascension. As Jesus leaves the earth, he has equipped them through what he has communicated. Due to his person, divine and human, his authoritative words struck the disciples' hearts to obey him.

---

[72] Chris Shirley, "It Takes a Church to Make a Disciple: An Integrative Model of Discipleship for the Local Church," *Southwestern Journal of Theology* 50, no. 2 (2008): 209.

[73] John 6:39.

[74] John 2:19.

[75] Matthew 16:22.

The disciples are to teach others all that Jesus taught. How and why Jesus communicated were to be transferred as part of Jesus teaching for all to observe. The reason to train the local church to make disciples becomes clear, which is because of Jesus and all that he represents, does, reveals, and is. The clarity stems from Jesus' communicating to his disciples. Remove Jesus' communication and one removes the ability to learn about Jesus or making disciples.

Example by Jesus' Life

The gospels[76] reveal to each pastor that Jesus is dynamic in his person and works. Pastors are to study, learn, live, and teach the many aspects of the gospels to the local church. Since Jesus dwelt on the earth among people, he did more than just verbalize a message or communicate. What, how, and why Jesus spoke parallels his actions or his works. What are some examples of Jesus' works that inspire a pastor to train and invite the

---

[76] Matthew, Mark, Luke and John

local church to make disciples? The following three categories will help shape the answer: (1) Jesus' Prayer; (2) Jesus' Relationships; and (3) Jesus' Death and Resurrection.

Jesus' Prayer

Jesus set an example of a genuine relationship with the Father for his followers to witness and mimic. As Jesus was on the earth, he revealed this relationship to the Father through his communication and also his prayer life. Jesus continued a faithful prayer life among the disciples, especially nearing the end of his earthly ministry. Jesus petitioned the Father for the advance of his mission, guidance for his disciples,[77] and salvation of the world.[78] Jesus' prayer reveals his desire and mediatory actions for his disciples. Jesus' prayer validated his verbal message that he desired to make disciples and train those disciples to make disciples.

---

[77] John 17:9.
[78] John 17:2.

Prayer was not a ministry or program, but a relational aspect of communication that derived out of sincerity. Though Jesus might have prayed at certain places and times, a pastor must see the priority of relationship causes the purposeful nature of prayer to God the Father. Through that sincerity, interaction, and involvement of others, people are trained to be in relationship to God – not fulfilling a programmatic duty. Even fasting was a gut, convictional response of lacking the desire to eat versus a structured purpose to cause spirituality or closeness with God. Jesus' fast of 40 days[79] had correlation to the Old Testament story of Noah and the flood as it rained 40 days and 40 nights.[80] As God sustained Noah, so will Jesus be sustained[81] – especially that of temptation by Satan to sin. Even so, a person's actions do not create closeness with God (like fasting or prayer) nor is it right for anyone to base their prayer life off of feelings (i.e. "I don't feel close to

---

[79] Matthew 4:2; Mark 1:13; and Luke 4:2.

[80] Genesis 7:4.

[81] Matthew 4:1 "Jesus was led up by the Spirit."

God."). Prayer life is generated from two things: 1) God creating the avenue for his creation to communicate to him and 2) a right relationship with him through the mediator Jesus empowered by the Spirit.

Want people to pray? Guide them to a relationship to God and the Spirit will convict and guide them to pray.[82] Want them to be genuine? Be genuine. Want them to know? Then teach them, by word and deed.

Jesus' Relationships

Jesus placed himself in situations to make disciples, thus training his disciples to make disciples. These situations differed from the law-abiding Jews, scribes and Pharisees, in which they believed certain people in Israel deserved rejection.[83] God evidently opposed this rejection and revealed his love for all nations and people.[84] By setting himself in a position to

---

[82] Romans 8:26; Ephesians 6:18; Philippians 1:19; and Jude 20.
[83] Mark 2:16; John 4:9.
[84] Acts 10:28; Ephesians 2:11-22.

communicate and even dine with unbelievers, he was revealing himself to them in order to bring them into relationship with him. Since Jesus is truth and the only way for people to know of God is through truth, Jesus delivered the truth to the people through himself.[85] Jesus reveals that building relationship with unbelievers makes disciples and trains disciples to do likewise.

There's several sticky, difficult points for pastors and relationships. Often relationships are superficial as often people's character over the course of life reveal themselves untrustworthy. As pastors share deep things of their life, it can been weaponized against them whether directly or indirectly, especially publically. Gossip and slander ensue and pastors stick behind a threshold of boundaries, often rightly so.

Still yet, Jesus exemplified a relationship to all types of people but he never swayed from his mission, message, and identity. Therefore, the pastor needs to be secure in his identity and relationship to

---

[85] John 14:6.

Christ to be led by wisdom in dealing with people. From relationship to God, pastors learn to be loved even when the world around them is entirely unloving. More so, they learn to love those that are unloving in which they had been. We see this entirely in Jesus' relationships to his disciples that became apostles, his disciples that were women from various backgrounds (i.e. demon possessed), crowds, Jewish leaders, Roman government, poor and needy, and diseased.

When pastors stick with one-man show, they keep walls high and thick against people or wide-open without discernment and wisdom – creating an exhausting relational network. When pulpit preachers stay behind pulpits and office doors, they leave a veiled perception of spirituality and genuineness void of authentic relationships. When pastors follow trends, they can begin compromising truths and re-defining love to retain attention by people and the masses. When pastors stick with traditions, they elevate traditions over God and the gospel and allow for relational prison of keeping people in and keeping people out. The implications and applications are innumerable for pastors and their relationships to Christians and non-Christians (which they were once before in their own life).

Want people to make disciples? Want people to trust in Christ? Want the church to be followers of him and engaged relationally to those around them in real life? Walk with Christ as his disciple, a Christian. Treat others as Jesus did and does. Teach them Jesus. Don't want anything out of them like what they might give you or even take away. They are not a product, price tag, pew filler, or potential enemy. See people through God's eyes and discover immense amount of guidance and wisdom to deal with all kinds of people and situations.

Jesus' Death and Resurrection

Jesus' death and resurrection serves as the greatest reason for a pastor to train the local church to make disciples. Jesus supplied the disciple's life through his physical death and resurrection, ensuring making disciples process continues. Since Jesus desired to depart from the earth, he left the gospel proclamation to the disciples, and to the disciples of the disciples.[86] By his death and resurrection, Jesus trained the disciples to love and die for others.[87] Jesus' earthly life ended ultimately in his death, resurrection, and ascension, fulfilling the Father's will. It ultimately validates Jesus' mission and message to make disciples, in which his disciples were to deny[88] themselves, take up their cross, and follow.[89] Following Jesus means to listen, trust, and obey him, even imitate. As Jesus obeyed the Father and his mission, everyone is to obey and follow God's mission. Out of the person and work of Jesus flows the reason to train, the reason to imitate Jesus' example in obedience to his teaching.

---

[86] Acts 1:8.

[87] John 15:13.

[88] Luke 9:23 context shows us that "deny" refers to a re-focus on someone else beyond ourselves. Therefore, focus on Jesus. This is different that "denial" as if it's a health-related diet, religions belief system of removing life's pleasures, or even harming oneself so the mind and body are in complete subjection. Jesus' point to his disciples was that the Son of Man will be the one lifted up on the cross for the world to believe and follow.

[89] Mark 8:34 and Luke 9:23.

Often in real life, pastors can sense lifelessness, purposeless, and even failure throughout the years. The thrill of the gospel seems to fade and the pastoral task loses glory. Temptations arise to be jealous of other pastors "success" spiritually, numerical growth in a church, compensation, and so on. The gospel wanes as the central, glorious issue to behold personally, relationally, and corporately.

These struggles only reveal the necessity and relevance of the gospel even more. They reveal an opportunity for spiritual growth and understanding of what God has done two thousand years prior to the difficult struggle of one's week of pastoral failures. Even when pastors sense the local church lifeless, then they may very well be discerning what needs to be addressed.

Instead of being concerned of blowback and resistance, pastors must heed their chief shepherd and his good news. Jesus is the reason to be a disciple let alone make and train disciples. One of the hardest things for pastors is loss and surviving rejection. Pastors must take in Jesus' words more deeply and remember that Jesus was murdered!

If pastors are concerned for how others think of them, then that is a trap and snare Satan and sin will use to diminish the gospel. Instead of Christian pastors living and preaching "unashamed of the gospel,"[90] they talk and walk to gain the world's glory instead of God's glory. The relational, spiritual, physical, familial, and financial pressures are enormous but so is God and the gospel – hence Paul's words to be "steadfast" and "immovable."[91]

If pastors feel the strain, just think of the local church and their strain each week in all courses of life. Pastors can truly learn about their people by even enduring the same difficulties of the local church. Often pastors are already experienced in these things and come ready to speak and serve in these life situations. Pastors can learn to grieve loss while being spiritually fueled by the Spirit and God's word. Jesus never trained his

---

[90] Romans 1:16.
[91] 1 Corinthians 15:58.

disciples to be stupid in the world but rather "wise as serpents and innocent as doves."[92]

Pastors can live financially wise though not greedy. They can be relationally stable though not used or using others. They can be spiritually alive when the world around them is dead though often tempted to distrust and lose heart. They can gain godliness of character, mind, and heart though rejected and reviled. There is a way for the pastor to succeed and his name is Jesus.

---

[92] Matthew 10:16.

CHAPTER 4
TRAINING TO MAKE DISCIPLES BECAUSE OF JESUS' REDEMPTION

Until a pastor is both redeemed by Jesus and understands the implications of the redemption, training the local church to make disciples will be "clear as mud." If a pastor is in this to get or gain anything, then it will be revealed as such and be marked by lovelessness, pride, etc.

In 1 Timothy, Paul trained Timothy in a different way than some leaders were acting.[93] Paul trained Timothy to pastor out of being loved by God which results in loving others. Without God, there's no truth or love and certainly no gospel or redemption. Pastors do not become redeemed in order to pastor as if to get

---

[93] C.f. 1 Timothy 1:1-5 and 6:1-12.

something (e.g. pay, prestige, popularity, power), rather, pastors shepherd because they are redeemed from sin, themselves, the world, and living without God.

Instead of using people, they pastor them. Instead of seeing people as givers, they give of themselves. Instead of appeasing people, they live trusting God is pleased with them. Instead of becoming hardened by the world, they become humbled by God. Instead of living by the weighty pressures of ministry and life, they learn to live by the weight of God's glory. Instead of falling prey to legalism or licentiousness, they live liberated to follow God. Instead of being a yes man or no man, they learn to say yes to God and no to the world. Instead of living by their personality, they live transformed by God.

In Colossians, Paul even explains the connection between redemption[94] and the whole church participating

---

[94] Set free from sin, mainly referring to the "release from a captive condition" from ἀπολύτρωσις. *A Greek-English Lexicon of the New Testament and Other Early Christian Literature*, 3rd ed., ed. Frederick William Danker (Chicago: The University of Chicago, 2000), 117.

in making disciples outlined in the following: (1) Paul knows the church to be "bearing fruit and growing" after hearing the gospel from another disciple;[95] (2) Paul prays for the church to "be filled with the knowledge of his will in all spiritual wisdom and understanding,"[96] which comes from Jesus' teaching and example; (3) Paul prays so that the wisdom and understanding guides them "to walk in a manner worthy of the Lord,"[97] a manner that Jesus set for all His disciples while on the earth; (4) Paul reminds the church of its present and future salvation coming from Jesus' redemption, forgiving the church member's sins;[98] (5) Paul assures them Jesus is still head over the church,[99] in which the church is to submit to his teaching and example; (6) Paul assures the church that Jesus desires to "reconcile"[100] people to him through his

---

[95] Colossians 1:6.

[96] Colossians 1:9.

[97] Colossians 1:10.

[98] Colossians 1:14.

[99] Colossians 1:18.

[100] "The restoration to friendship and fellowship after estrangement ... When an individual heart sees and trusts in the value of

death and resurrection – the gospel message,[101] insinuating that the church must not be lax in obedience to make disciples; (7) Paul is a "minister" of this gospel, a pastor training the church;[102] (8) Paul reminds them that Jesus desires to "make known" to Gentiles the gospel[103] and (9) Paul is to share with the church in making known the gospel to everyone.[104] Both Paul and the church at Colossae are beneficiaries of Jesus' teaching, example and his obedient disciples making known the gospel. Paul, a pastor in this situation, affirms that the ministry of making known the gospel to everyone involves everyone in the local church. The church, along with Paul, is to make known or reveal the gospel to all peoples, even the Gentiles.

Christ's atoning death, he becomes reconciled to God, hostility is removed, friendship and fellowship eventuate." Merrill F. Unger, *Unger's Bible Dictionary* (Chicago, IL: Moody, 1966), 914.

[101] Colossians 1:20.

[102] Colossians 1:23.

[103] Colossians 1:27.

[104] Colossians 1:28.

From this short, outlined example showing the connection from redemption to the whole church, the following chapter entails a short, concise outline to clarify the connection. The outline is as follows: (1) Jesus Redeems a Pastor and (2) Jesus Redeems a Pastor's Mission. As one may conclude, the outline reveals a primary focus on Jesus redeeming the whole of a pastor's life and pastoral job description, versus compartmentalizing the effectiveness of Jesus' redemption to a particular area of life.

Jesus Redeems a Pastor

Because of Paul being redeemed by Jesus, he now serves Jesus in a role[105] and function[106] in the church, as an apostle with shepherding and oversight. Paul is known as an apostle,[107] and he sets forth commands,

---

[105] C.f. 1 Timothy 3:1, "office" (ἐπισκοπῆς). "Engagement in oversight, supervision, of leaders of Christian communities." *BDAG*, 379.

[106] Referring to "member" (μέλη) of the body. C.f. 1 Corinthians 12:1-14.

[107] Colossians 1:1.

wisdom and guidance for training the local church. Paul creates a connection between a pastor's redeemed life directly to the pastor's philosophy of ministry. By so doing Paul reveals every part of a pastor's life hinges on the teachings and examples of Jesus, including a pastor's local church ministry.

Redeemed Relationship to Jesus

For pastors to begin any sort of ministry, they are to believe and obey Jesus. Thus, a pastor must first seek individual redemption before serving among the church, which is the corporate aspect of Jesus' redemption. Jesus desires to affect both the pastor as well as the church. However, before a pastor is able to affect the church, Jesus must first affect him.

Paul claims many times throughout the New Testament the importance of true, genuine faith in Jesus as the beginning place for any work that God deems good. For example, Paul states to the church in Ephesus that they were once dead[108] but made alive by God.[109] He made them alive by Jesus' death and resurrection.[110] Specifically, a person is made alive by having faith in him.[111] When doing so, that person becomes his workmanship, created to do good works.[112] Therefore, in order to do a qualified good work, like making disciples or training others to do so, one must have faith in Jesus.

Prayer

With a pastor redeemed by having faith in Jesus, he now has access to God and, specifically, access to talking to him. Prayer is the result of a believer's new relationship to God. Upon having faith in Jesus for redemption and forgiveness of sin, a believer is recognized and treated as one of God's children.[113] A

---

[108] Ephesians 2:1.

[109] Ephesians 2:4.

[110] Ephesians 2:5-7.

[111] Ephesians 2:8.

[112] Ephesians 2:10.

[113] Romans 8:15.

pastor is not alone in ministry, and even more so, God is listening to his needs and wants. Even Jesus taught[114] and modeled[115] prayer. Prayer offers the pastor help in life issues and allows him to align himself humbly to God's will. As the pastor prays transparently[116] and towards what God desires, the pastor's heart becomes malleable for God to form. He then will form the heart into loving what he loves, such as people, and more specifically, training the local church to make disciples. An honest prayer from a pastor to God would reveal the pastor's inability to carry on ministry alone and as the only capable person. Rather, the pastor needs to recognize God works through every believer to make disciples.

---

[114] Matthew 6:9.

[115] John 17.

[116] Versus a façade or assumed spiritual pride before God, as in denying thoughts or actions that are occurring that may need forgiveness.

Reading the Word

From faith to prayer, reading God's Word provides incredible comfort and direction for a pastor. The author of Hebrews describes God's words, being what created the earth,[117] are invisible but amazingly powerful. If God's words created the heavens and the earth, then God's Word will surely guide a pastor in a ministry.

Paul describes the scriptures as "God breathed,"[118] in "which are able to make you wise for salvation through faith in Christ Jesus."[119] Paul affirms to Timothy that having faith in Jesus will enable him to be wise, guiding Him to use God's Word for "training in righteousness."[120] God desires each believer to be "equipped for every good work."[121] Paul has set in place the reason for Jesus, faith, good works and God's Word.

---

[117] Heb. 11:3.
[118] 2 Timothy 3:16.
[119] 2 Timothy 3:15.
[120] 2 Timothy 3:16.
[121] 2 Timothy 3:17.

Jesus redeems the pastor to have faith in him. From this faith flows good works that are guided by God's Word, powerful enough to change the pastor's life just as they are to create the heavens and the earth.[122]

Redeemed Relationship to Sin

A pastor lacks the ability to be perfect as Jesus and still exists in sinful flesh until death.[123] The pastor will assuredly deal with his own sin; however, he will deal with sin with the indwelling Spirit[124] and the power of God's Word[125] to assist him in conviction, confession, repentance, and healing. The pastor displaying a façade of a perfect life reveals the lack of need for Jesus, his forgiveness, and his redemption. Pastors are to walk in a manner resembling the truth and humble thanks for Jesus' merciful redemption, as Paul

---

[122] Genesis 1:1.
[123] Romans 7:21-25.
[124] Romans 8:13.
[125] Romans 1:16.

states to Timothy.[126] As pastors believe and act accordingly, they will understand Jesus' perspective on the world, and begin treating the world as Jesus did, for which he gave His life!

Redeemed Relationship to the World

Following redemption and the biblical understanding of how God treats the pastor as his child, the pastor is commanded to imitate Jesus' teaching and example. A pastor's life, especially his ministry, must contain both the verbalized message of the gospel and transformed living example that validates the message. If not, the pastor dissolves into hypocritical, duplicitous, untrustworthy, acting, and more.

The pastor's only distinguishing difference from the local church is his particular role and function. He still is a human, a sinner saved by grace, one living by faith, and one always in need of Jesus. From this perspective, a pastor possesses no right to be prideful or

---

[126] 1 Timothy 1:12-17.

arrogant, whether in life or specifically in ministry. As a pastor acts according to Jesus' attitude,[127] he will recognize that the world, regardless of disgusting sin,[128] needs to hear the gospel message.

From a humble attitude, Jesus taught and exemplified to the world who he is and the necessity to believe in him. His humility revealed reverence and relationship to God the Father, which defines humility to live with the recognition someone else is exalted.[129] Humility then is the personal characteristic from one's position or vantage-point. Jesus came to serve God the Father and the world, but this serving is not catering, placating, pandering, politicizing, posturing, but rather a pastoring (shepherding) to someone. Humility is receptive, instructive, and directional. Humility serves all by serving one. Humility is what Jesus describes as "good soil"[130] which is receptive to the seed of God's

---

[127] Philippians 2:5.
[128] 1 Timothy 1:8-11.
[129] John 17 and Philippians 2:5.
[130] Luke 8:1-15.

word but nonetheless hard to anything else. Humility receives like a learning child of the direction to go and the direction to avoid. Humility will say yes to one thing and say no to thousands of things. Humility is not weakness but receptivity to God and his strength. Humility is not wimpiness but worship. Humility is not cowardice but courage. Humility discerns when to listen, speak, and take action. Humility is not a dead, undiscerning sheep but alive to see the world and the word for what it is. Humility learns truth and transforms to love the object (God) in which is at work to plant in the good soil of the heart. Humility becomes a mark of the Christian, especially that of the Christian pastor following the chief shepherd Jesus.

    Only a humble attitude sees the need to make disciples accordingly, especially in training the local church to make disciples. Jesus humbly trained his disciples to continue the work of the ministry. Pastors reveal a prideful attitude by solely doing the work of making disciples or the absence thereof. Pride is hard-heartedness to God and his word. Pride is God-lessness. Pride is sin, and sin ultimately is that which is not of

God. Sin is Christlessness. Sinful people are to be redeemed, redeemed to serve Christ Jesus since Jesus died for the sinners[131] and ungodly[132] hence why the gospel is good news to the world!

Through Jesus facing death, he trained his disciples to give their lives to God, and in so doing, give their lives to the world in proclaiming to them Jesus' teaching and example.[133]

Though humble, Jesus didn't teach for his disciples to learn, teach, or train others to be unwise or ignorant.[134] Jesus taught discernment both verbally and through his actions. For example, Jesus discerned that many Pharisees, who were arrogantly opposed to him as the Messiah and Son of God, needed strong verbal rebuke of their failure to obey God[135] and physically overturned the money changers tables.[136] As pastors deal

---

[131] Luke 15:7.
[132] Romans 5:6-8.
[133] Luke 9:23.
[134] Matthew 10:16.
[135] Matthew 23:27.
[136] John 2:15.

with people in this world, they are redeemed from making erroneous, ignorant decisions as in ignoring making or training disciples. If they have done so, they are also, humbly, in a position to receive forgiveness or help from God in the situation.

Jesus Redeems a Pastor's Mission

As a pastor reflects on Jesus redeeming him, it is then the connection between Jesus' teaching and example becomes first and foremost the template for the pastor's ministry. The pastor is the beneficiary of the process Jesus put into place through his teaching and example. Having listened to Jesus' teaching, watched his example and now personally experienced the redemption, the pastor possesses two main responsibilities. First, as a believer, the pastor is to make disciples as one did of him. Second, as in the spiritual gift, role, and function, the pastor is to train the church in and by Jesus' teaching and example, so as to equip them in doing the ministry. Ministry is defined not by organizational structures or program schedules, but literally how to do and deal with real life (jobs, skills, issues, sins, people, parenting, etc.) because of God and the gospel.

Make Disciples

Regarding the first responsibility for a pastor as a believer, Marshall and Payne offer an accurate and healthy rebuke to those not aligned to Jesus' teaching and example. They write, "We have to conclude that a Christian with no passion for the lost is in serious need of self-examination and repentance."[137] For pastors, a passion and love for the lost is central to the gospel, which is to be central in ministry. If God gave his life[138] for those that never knew him,[139] then how much more is called of a pastor? Paul informs Timothy of the aim or direction of their ministry, which is love.[140] Paul further

---

[137] Colin and Payne Marshal, Tony, *The Trellis and the Vine* (Kingsford, NSW: Matthias Media, 2009), 52.

[138] John 3:16.

[139] Romans 3:10.

[140] 1 Timothy 1:5.

develops the idea of love in the context of ministry throughout the remaining chapters, especially the first chapter. In so doing, Paul rebukes those teachers using the law in an unhelpful, unloving and misdirected way.[141] Paul uses his personal testimony of redemption to direct Timothy in the right direction in ministry.[142] Timothy learns that Paul is the beneficiary of Jesus' love for unbelievers.[143] Jesus called Paul into the ministry of proclaiming the gospel to the world.[144] Paul listened to Jesus' teaching and watched his example, which then became the template for loving people and making them disciples.[145] Replacing such an aim (telos)[146] or mission in a pastor's ministry could be idolatrous, misdirected, unloving or, in many cases, misinformed.

---

[141] 1 Timothy 1:8.

[142] 1 Timothy 1:12.

[143] 1 Timothy 1:14-15.

[144] 1 Timothy 1:12, 16.

[145] 1 Timothy 1:16. C.f. Marshall and Payne offer additional clarity and analogies to suite this situation. Marshal, *The Trellis and the Vine*, 71.

[146] Telos is the English transliteration of the Greek word for τέλος found in 1 Timothy 1:5 for "aim" or "goal."

Train Others to Make Disciples

Regarding the second responsibility for a pastor as in the role and function, Marshall and Payne offer additional and extremely helpful insight. They state in reflecting on Paul's commands for Timothy to "train yourself for godliness" in 1 Timothy 4:7, "The focus here is on teaching and example, leading to a particular character of life rather than to a particular skill or competency."[147] The authors concluded that Paul's training of Timothy revolved around imitation and relationship to each other versus "a barren, educational exercise."[148] Basically, Jesus did not train based on people's need of a skill set, as in academic, seminary training. Rather, the reason is found within the gospel, which is teaching and exemplifying to the world who Jesus is, their need of Jesus and what Jesus teaches. Being redeemed, a pastor is now capable of seeing and understanding that a pastor's mission primarily focuses

---

[147] Ibid., 72.

[148] Ibid., 71-72.

on two responsibilities (1) making disciples and (2) training the local church to make disciples. Of which, both have been taught and exemplified by Jesus Christ himself.

George Barna, a Christian researcher of church and pastor trends, states: "Keep your eyes on the goal: We are dedicated to producing genuine followers of Jesus Christ."[149] Followers are disciple-making disciples. To further clarify:

> The method of Jesus here was more than a continuous sermon; it was an object lesson ... His training classes were never dismissed. How else will his way ever be learned? It is good to tell people what we mean, but it is infinitely better to show them. People are looking for a demonstration, not an explanation. When it is all boiled down, those of us who are seeking to train people must be prepared to have them follow us,

---

[149] George Barna, *Growing True Disciples New Strategies for Producing Genuine Followers of Christ* (Colorado Springs, CO: Waterbrook, 2001), 132.

even as we follow Christ[150] ... There can be no shirking or evading of our personal responsibility to show the way to those we are training, and this revelation must include the practical outworking in life of the deeper realities of the Spirit. This is the Master's method, and nothing else will ever suffice to train others to do his work.[151]

---

[150] 1 Corinthians 11:1.

[151] Coleman, *The Master Plan of Discipleship*, 68.

CHAPTER 5
CONCLUSION

From Jesus flows his teaching and example, revealing a humble life in serving and dying for unbelieving people of the world across generations and geography. He commissioned his disciples and those following likewise to live a life parallel to his through belief and obedience to him. Being a primary example of belief and obedience, Paul set a pattern of making disciples and training others to make disciples through men such as Timothy. From the primary examples of Jesus and Paul, a pastor can confidently conclude that the primary goal for a pastor is being given to the church to ensure the world knows Jesus through training the local church to make disciples by the pastor's teaching and example.

Implications for a Pastor's Teaching

A pastor trains the local church through both his example and teaching. Particularly, his teaching will reflect his beliefs and convictions. The means, content, and audience of his teaching will best reflect the pastor's convictions, which reflect the pastor's understanding of Jesus' teaching and example.

A pastor is to use God's word (the Bible) correctly as a source by which he studies, teaches, and lives.[152] By God's word, he is to put himself in a position that best attests to making disciples. A pastor's authentic understanding of Jesus arises in the face of his followers, specifically the local church. A pastor solely focused on using the pulpit as a means for teaching evidences a lack of understanding of Jesus, though fulfilling a particular means of teaching in feeding the flock.

A pastor's heart and mind aligned to Jesus will seek out people. Jesus and the disciples used means of a house, field, lake, garden, synagogue, etc. in seeking

---

[152] Matthew 4:4; 2 Timothy 2:15.

out people to teach. For a pastor to be limited to a Sunday school room or the pulpit to which people must come rather than the pastor going to them, seems unparalleled to Jesus' teaching and example.

As a pastor questions which means to use in order to make disciples and train the local church to do likewise, the particular audience of listeners comes into light. In choosing or not choosing a certain audience to teach, a pastor reveals his true heart as whether aligned to Jesus or not. Jesus spoke with the rejected people of his day, like tax collectors, prostitutes and Samaritans. A pastor is to open his eyes to the rejected people of his day in order to teach and make disciples. Even so in a Sunday school room or pulpit, a pastor is to be concerned for them as people rather than filling them with data such as computer data entry or an angry father rebuking his children to follow his class-room rules.

Applications for a Pastor's Example

A pastor is an example to the local church by what he does, which comes from who he is. By who he is as well as what he does becomes an example for the local church. He is able to train the church, alike to Jesus, through being an example. Perfection is not the key, rather, "striving"[153] towards and directing others to Jesus is to be the pattern. If the pastor sets the tone of spiritual health of being perfect, then his church most likely follows suit. Perfection only comes through Jesus' redemption rather than one's ability to achieve any moralistic or legalistic standard.

    A pastor's attitude begins revealing his true understanding of Jesus' teaching and example. As many come around the pastor, they begin to perceive who he is, such as arrogant, prideful, or even demeaning. Many times, these can be subtle for a pastor. Arrogance is revealed when lifting up one's own ministry by tearing down another local ministry in what they are failing at, rather than seeking ways for that church to change, such as Jesus directed to the seven churches in Revelation 2-3. Pride manifests itself through the rejection of serving

---

[153] Marshal, *The Trellis and the Vine*, 74.

alongside certain local churches that differ in doctrine, rather than seeking unity in Jesus, though there does need to be boundaries of some kind. Demeaning arrives through making fun of unbelievers in the midst of teaching or around the dinner table for their lack of understanding of particular teachings of Jesus or lack of obedience. All such pastoral attitudes deter rather than direct people to Jesus or training his church to do likewise.

For organized pastors, observing their calendars and schedules reveals whether or not they are striving to make disciples or training to do so. The schedule can pertain to family events and occasions or the structure of the ministry calendar and events. Adjusting the schedule to include events such as meals, walks, working out, trips, etc. to include being with people to teach them about Jesus or train them will serve as an immediate application.

Those with which the pastor meets sheds immense light on his understanding for the reason to train the local church to make disciples. For a pastor not to associate himself with a sinner who needs Jesus calls into question his knowledge of Jesus' teaching and especially his example. Many things can prevent a pastor from associating with such people like the following: (1) being comfortable with close friends at church, never wanting to expand; (2) seeing people as a bother to his schedule; (3) a frustration for someone's inability to do their job over the counter at a certain store; and even (4) happy in only attending pastors conferences rather than his son's soccer game with hundreds of unbelievers in attendance. Let it be a redeemed pastor's heart to both make and train to make disciples through his teaching and example!

What do pastors want people to be – churchy or Christian? What do pastors want people to be – disciples of life or disciples of Jesus? What do pastors want people to be – blind to the world or wisely dealing with the world? What do pastors want for people – what pastors want for the church and communities or what God wants?

When a pastor makes disciples of Jesus, he trains them to live soundly in this chaotic world God loves.

BIBLIOGRAPHY

A Greek-English Lexicon of the New Testament and Other Early Christian Literature. 3rd ed., ed. Frederick William Danker. Chicago: The University of Chicago, 2000.

Barna, George. *Growing True Disciples New Strategies for Producing Genuine Followers of Christ*. Colorado Springs, CO: Waterbrook, 2001.

Begg, Derek Prime and Alistair. *On Being a Pastor: Understanding Our Calling and Work*. Chicago, IL: Moody, 2004.

Bingham, D. Jeffrey. *Pocket History of the Church*. Downers Grove, IL: Intervarsity, 2002.

Clowney, Edmund P. *The Church*. Downers Grove, IL: Intervarsity, 1995.

Coleman, Robert E. *The Master Plan of Discipleship*. Old Tappan, N.J.: Revell, 1987.

Cordeiro, Robert Lewis and Wayne. *Culture Shift Transforming Your Church from the inside Out*. San Francisco, CA: Jossey-Bass, 2005.

Gonzalez, Justo L. *The Early Church to the Dawn of the Reformation*. Vol. 1. 3 vols. The Story of Christianity. New York, NY: Harper Collins, 1984.

Hoehner, Harold W. *Ephesians an Exegetical Commentary*. Grand Rapids, MI: Baker, 2002.

MacArthur, John. *Pastoral Ministry: What Is a Pastor to Be and Do?* Nashville, TN: Thomas Nelson, 2005.

Marshal, Colin and Payne, Tony. *The Trellis and the Vine*. Kingsford, NSW: Matthias Media, 2009.

Shirley, Chris. "It Takes a Church to Make a Disciple: An Integrative Model of Discipleship for the Local Church." *Southwestern Journal of Theology* 50, no. 2 (2008): 207-24.

Unger, Merrill F. *Unger's Bible Dictionary*. Chicago, IL: Moody, 1966.

Wilkins, Michael J. *Following the Master a Biblical Theology of Discipleship*. Grand Rapids, MI: Zondervan, 1992.

_____. *The NIV Application Commentary: Matthew*, ed. Terry Muck. Grand Rapids, MI: Zondervan, 2004.

ABOUT THE AUTHOR

Mr. Nate is married to Abby and they have 7 kids (4 girls and 3 boys). He grew up in the Sacramento, CA region at Valley Christian Academy (Roseville, CA). He degreed with a B.A. in Biblical Studies at The Master's University (Santa Clarita, CA) and Th.M. in Educational Leadership at Dallas Theological Seminary (Dallas, TX).

He has worked in various capacities since he was a kid, and he has experienced various jobs providing a unique perspective to real life: janitorial, construction, plumbing, athletics, food service, equestrian therapy, shipping and logistics, customer service, sales, travel, international student education, real estate, system and database development, teacher, and pastor.

He authors Mr. Nate Books, an illustrated kid's and educational book collection. Information about the author and book collections can be found online at MrNateBooks.com.

www.ingramcontent.com/pod-product-compliance
Lightning Source LLC
Chambersburg PA
CBHW071412290426
44108CB00014B/1794